TECHNOLOGY IN TIMES PAST

Ancient China

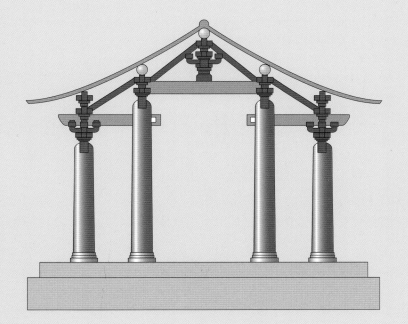

ROBERT SNEDDEN

A⁺

Smart Apple Media

Smart Apple Media is published by Black Rabbit Books
P.O. Box 3263, Mankato, Minnesota 56002

Printed in China

Library of Congress Cataloging-in-Publication Data

Snedden, Robert.
    Ancient China / Robert Snedden.
    p. cm. — (Smart apple media— technology in times past)
    Includes index.
    Summary: "Covers the inventions and technology used in Ancient China and how their ideas influenced technology today"—Provided by publisher.
    ISBN 978-1-59920-298-3
    1. Technology—China—History—Juvenile literature. 2. China—Civilization—Juvenile literature. I. Title.
T16.S63 2009
609.31—dc22

2007050041

Designed by Helen James
Edited by Pip Morgan
Illustrations by Graham Rosewarne
Picture research by Su Alexander

Picture acknowledgements
Page 3 Louis Laurent Grandadam/Corbis; 4 Vince Streano/Corbis; 6 Goebel/Zefa/Corbis; 7 Keren Su/Corbis; 8 Redlink/Corbis; 10 Golestan Palace Teheran/Gianni Dagli Orti/The Art Archive; 11 Karl Goh/EPA/Corbis; 12 Christie's Images/Corbis; 13t Keren Su/Corbis, b Mario Anzuoni/Corbis; 15t Sylvan Barnet & William Burto Collection/The Art Archive, b Bob Krist/Corbis; 16 Bohemian Nomad Picturemakers/Corbis; 17 British Library/The Art Archive; 18 Christie's Images/Corbis; 19 Mike McQueen/Corbis; 20 Burstein Collection/Corbis; 21 Asian Art & Archaeology, Inc./Corbis; 22 Galerie Delalande Louvre des Antiquaires/Gianni Dagli Orti/The Art Archive; 23 DBImages/Alamy; 25 Reza; Webistan/Corbis; 26 Stock Connection Distribution/Alamy; 27 Arco Images/Alamy; 28 Bibliotheque Nationale Paris/The Art Archive; 29 Nik Wheeler/Corbis; 30 Charles & Josette Lenars/Corbis; 31 Roger Ressmeyer/Corbis; 32 Maxine Adcock/Science Photo Library; 33t Bruce Burkhardt/Corbis, b Private Collection/ Marc Charmet/The Art Archive; 34 Keren Su/Getty Images; 35 Yang Liu/Corbis

Front cover Goebel/Zefa/Corbis

9 8 7 6 5 4 3 2 1

Contents

AN ANCIENT CIVILIZATION

China is one of the world's oldest and certainly most long-lasting civilizations. It has endured for more than 5,000 years, and today, China remains one of the world's most powerful countries. The people of ancient China were isolated from the other great civilizations and believed their land was the center of Earth.

ORDER IN HEAVEN

The rulers of China believed that their fortunes were dictated by events in heaven. This belief led to the rise of astronomy in China, so everything that went on in the sky was carefully observed and recorded. Thanks to the astronomers of ancient China, we have catalogs of stars and observations of events, such as comets, meteor showers, eclipses, and novae, that go back for several thousand years.

The earliest written records of ancient China have come from the Shang Dynasty (ca.1766–ca.1045 B.C.). These tell us that China was already a highly developed society known for

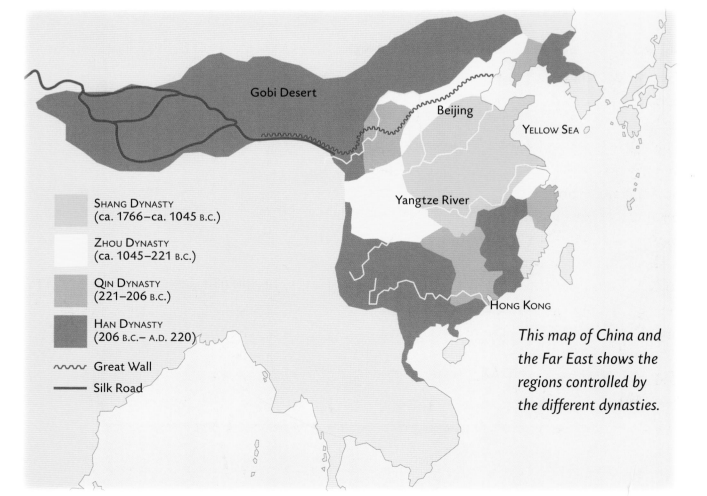

SHANG DYNASTY
(ca. 1766–ca. 1045 B.C.)

ZHOU DYNASTY
(ca. 1045–221 B.C.)

QIN DYNASTY
(221–206 B.C.)

HAN DYNASTY
(206 B.C.– A.D. 220)

∿∿∿ Great Wall

— Silk Road

This map of China and the Far East shows the regions controlled by the different dynasties.

its use of jade and bronze. The discovery of oracle bones, used for fortune telling and record keeping, show that the Chinese had a complex system of picture writing.

PRACTICAL PEOPLE

The ancient Chinese were very practical people who placed great value on their technological skills and achievements. They were always looking for ways to make improvements. For example, they found out how to smelt iron centuries before any other civilization. Their work in ceramics was the most accomplished in the world. The secret of making beautiful yet strong porcelain, known to the Chinese since around the seventh century A.D., was not discovered in Europe until almost a thousand years later.

THE FOUR GREAT INVENTIONS

The contributions that China has made to the world of science and technology are huge,

The emperors of China lived in the Forbidden City in Beijing. More than a million workers helped to build the palace during the early fifteenth century.

and we can only touch on some of them here. Four particular inventions, sometimes known as the Four Great Inventions of China, have changed the world. Paper provided a way to keep records and pass on ideas; and printing, using reusable type, made it easy to produce books in large numbers.

Gunpowder was accidentally discovered by alchemists looking for the secret of eternal life, but it changed warfare forever. The compass, first used to align homes in the luckiest direction, facing south, helped navigators steer their ships across the oceans. Without these inventions, civilization would have been very different.

Building Homes

Homes throughout ancient China had many things in common. These included building techniques using materials such as earth, timber, brick, and tiles. The design of houses was also similar, but varied according to people's wealth and the building materials that were available to them.

Building with the Earth

The earth has been a common building material in China for thousands of years. Today, substantial walls for a house are still made using the pounded earth technique.

This technique involved making a wooden frame into which earth was rammed down and pounded in order to form a wall. The best mixture to use contained 70 percent sand and 30 percent clay.

Effectively, the builders made artificial sandstone as they compressed the earth inside the frame. The wall was built much thicker at the bottom than at the top to give it stability. Once the wall was complete, the wooden frame was then removed and used again elsewhere.

Bricks are made in the traditional way and laid out on the ground at a brick-making factory in Kunming, China.

MAKING BRICKS

The earth was also used for making bricks. Usually, clay was shaped using wooden frames to make bricks of the required size. The bricks were either left to dry in the sun or baked in an oven to make them even harder. In some parts of China, after the crops had been harvested, bricks were cut directly from the fields and left to dry. This is still done today.

For major construction projects, such as building palaces, extra large bricks were often made. Some bricks that have been found were more than 1.5 feet (0.5 m) in length and weighed more than 110 pounds (50 kg).

The frame of a house included pillars and beams that supported the roof.

ROOF SUPPORT

The roofs of Chinese houses were made of heavy earthenware tiles. To support their weight, the Chinese invented a distinctive style of framing. Rather than the weight being supported only by the walls, as in European homes, the Chinese system used pillars and beams to hold up the roof. At the same time, this gave the designers and builders more choices for placing doors and windows in the walls.

UNDER-FLOOR HEATING

In colder parts of China, people slept on a raised platform called a *kang*. During the winter, the *kang* was warmed by hot air vents connected to stoves, providing a comfortable place to sleep. In the summer, the *kang* were fairly cool places.

FARMERS' CAVES

The farmers' caves of Shaanxi province in northern China are unique. Around 5,000 years ago, early settlers dug out shallow caves in natural earth holes in the mountains, strengthening them with wooden frames and lining them with grass and soil. They were warm in winter and cool in summer. People still live in these caves today.

THE GREAT WALL

The Great Wall of China is one of the largest construction projects ever. From east to west, the wall stretches for 1,500 miles (2,400 km). If the many side branches are included, the total length is about 4,500 miles (7,200 km). It is one of the modern wonders of the world.

JOINING THE WALLS

The Chinese built protective walls around their homes and settlements. Rival states built walls along their frontiers. The walls were made by the pounded earth method, with stones and twigs added for strength. In the third century B.C., under the first emperor of a united China, a number of existing walls were joined into a single system as protection against invading nomads from the north. This was the first Great Wall. Many hundreds of thousands of Chinese men worked under conditions of great hardship. Completing the work took around 10 years.

ANOTHER BRICK IN THE WALL

Much of the Great Wall was built with bricks. Brickmaking workshops, complete with kilns for firing the bricks, were set up along the wall. Bricks were more convenient for building than earth and stone because they were easy to make. Their small size and light weight meant that they were easy to transport to the places they were needed. The strength and durability of these bricks was just as good as anything we can make today.

The Jianyuguan Tower was built as a watchtower at the western end of the Great Wall.

The Great Wall of China (left), in the early evening light.

THE WALLS OF THE MING DYNASTY

Few traces now remain of these pounded earth walls. Most of the existing walls were built during China's Ming Dynasty in the fifteenth and sixteenth centuries A.D. The Ming had been defeated by the Mongols to the north and were eager to keep them out.

The early Ming walls were also built using the pounded earth method, but soon professional builders were building it with stone. The wall was not very effective. The Mongols either went around it or simply broke through. Stretches of the wall were often in need of repair.

The Great Wall that stands today is built of earth, stone, and brick. Its height ranges from 16 to 30 feet (5–9 m), with taller watch-towers spaced at regular intervals. It is 16 to 26 feet (5–8 m) wide, with a 13-foot (4-m) wide roadway running along the top that was intended for soldiers to march along.

FARMING THE LAND

There were farming communities in China as long ago as 5000 B.C. Their farming tools and techniques were more advanced than those in the West. Wheat was the main crop in northern China, while rice was the main crop in the south. People also grew millet, corn, barley, sweet potatoes, fruits, and vegetables.

IRON PLOWS

Stone plows at least 6,000 years old have been found in China. Wooden plows were most likely used too, but none have survived. A major development in Chinese farming was the iron plowshare around 600 B.C., about 500 years before it appeared in the West. Iron could easily be shaped to cut through the soil, and it has a good combination of strength and weight. An iron plow, pulled by oxen or water buffalo, was easier to use than a wooden one, and the plowing could be done much faster.

Around the first century B.C., the Chinese also invented the moldboard, which is a twisted plate above the plow that turns over the soil. European plows were made with moldboards several hundred years later.

Chinese farmers make terraces on the hillsides where they grow crops.

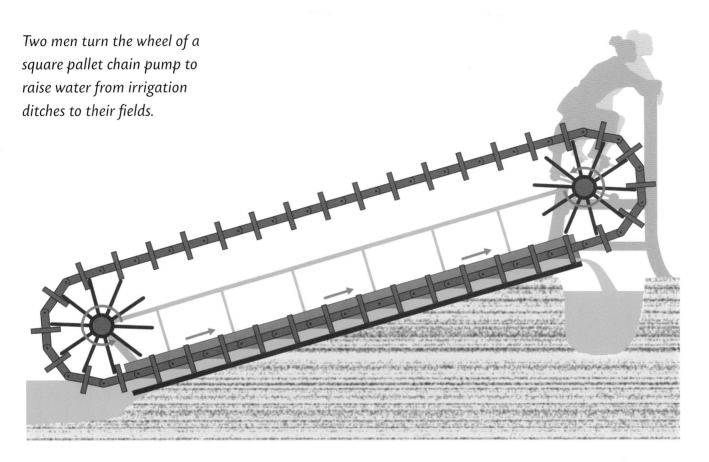

Two men turn the wheel of a square pallet chain pump to raise water from irrigation ditches to their fields.

ALL IN A ROW

Today, we see crops growing in fields in orderly rows that make them easier to tend and to harvest. But this is a fairly recent development in the West. Until the eighteenth century, European farmers sowed seeds by throwing them out in handfuls as they walked along a plowed field. However, in China, farmers were growing their crops in neat rows as early as the sixth century B.C.

WATERING THE LAND

Another useful Chinese invention was the square pallet chain pump for raising water from a lower level to a higher level to irrigate crops. It consisted of a number of wooden platforms, called pallets, that were attached to a continuous loop of chain. Turned by pedals, the pallets moving along the chain pulled up the water through a wooden channel and spilled it out at the top. A single pump could raise water about 13 feet (4 m).

THE WINNOWING FAN

After harvesting, the grain was separated from the unwanted parts of the plant, called the chaff. Traditionally, this was achieved by throwing the grain into the air so that the lighter chaff was blown away. The Chinese invented a rotary winnowing fan, cranked by hand, to speed up the process.

TEXTILES AND CLOTHES

The Chinese wove their garments from three main fibers: cotton, hemp, and silk. Textiles were created for many other purposes in ancient China. They were draped over chairs and tables, put on beds for warmth, hung on walls as decorations, made into book covers, and sewn into purses.

SPINNING FIBERS

People throughout the world have spun fibers into thread using a simple device called a drop spindle. This was little more than a weighted stick onto which a thread was spun as the spindle was dropped down. However, no one is sure when the spinning wheel first appeared. Some evidence suggests the Chinese used one in the sixth century A.D. What is certain is that Italian travelers brought it to Europe from China in the fourteenth century.

WEAVING ON LOOMS

Thread becomes cloth when it is woven on a loom. The discovery of fragments of fabric show that the Chinese had developed sophisticated weaving techniques by the eighteenth century B.C.

Chinese boys dressed in traditional uniforms leave an old academy after reenacting a classroom scene.

The earliest looms were probably invented in Egypt. These were made by hammering four pegs into the ground to form a rectangular frame; two crossbars across the frame held the threads. The weaver crouched down to operate the loom. The Chinese probably introduced foot treadles to lift the threads, making it much easier to weave the cloth.

The drawloom is thought to have been invented in China around the second century A.D. This allowed them to weave more intricate patterns by lifting specific groups of threads with different foot treadles.

A decoration on a Ming vase shows Chinese women weaving silk on a drawloom.

ANCIENT TEXTILES
In 2007, archaeologists made a discovery that is making people think again about the history of textiles in China. In a tomb dating to around 500 B.C., they found more than 20 pieces of fine silk, flax, and cotton cloth. The largest piece is 51 inches (130 cm) long and 20.5 inches (52 cm) wide and is woven using complicated techniques.

One piece of cotton was also found to have been dyed using vermilion, a red pigment made from the mineral cinnabar. The earliest records of vermilion being used before this find were from Arabia in the eighth century A.D., but the new discovery is more than a thousand years older.

15

SHIMMERING SILK

People in China have been producing silk for more than 5,000 years. Silk is an unusual fiber because it comes from the cocoon of the silkworm, which is the caterpillar of a type of moth. Clothes made of silk shimmer in the light. The Chinese kept the secret of silk production to themselves for more than 2,000 years.

This rare yellow silk robe was worn by a Chinese emperor. This Twelve Symbol Dragon Robe was made during the Qianlong Period (1736–1795).

SILK PRODUCTION

Producing silk is a time-consuming process that has changed little in thousands of years. The tiny eggs of the moth are kept in a warm place until they hatch. The silkworms that emerge are fed fresh mulberry leaves night and day. In a month, their weight increases up to 10,000 times.

Now the silkworms are ready to start spinning their cocoons, a task that takes them three to four days to complete. The cocoons are kept

warm and dry for eight to nine days and are then unwound. They are steamed to kill the caterpillar inside, then dipped in hot water to loosen the fibers. Each cocoon is formed from a single filament that can range in length from 1,970 to 2,950 feet (600–900 m).

Between five and eight cocoons are unwound at the same time, and the filaments are

THE SECRET GETS OUT

Around 550 A.D., silkworm eggs were smuggled from China to Byzantium (present-day Istanbul) by Persian monks. Silk production soon spread throughout Asia Minor and into Greece. When the Arabs invaded Persia (present-day Iran), they gained control of the thriving Persian silk industry. They spread the art of silk making across north Africa and into Spain and Sicily. By the thirteenth century, silk production had become established in Italy and eventually in the rest of Europe.

Round, shallow baskets contain thousands of silkworms producing silk.

Talkshow host Tyra Banks wears a shimmering silk dress at a ceremony in 2007.

twisted together to make a single thread of silk that is wound onto a spool. To make stronger threads, several single threads may be wound together using a spooling frame. The silk can then be woven into a cloth that is both lightweight and beautiful.

THE SILK SEASON

In the silk-producing areas of China, the women of almost every family devoted six months of the year to producing silk—from tending silkworms and unwinding the silk to spinning, weaving, dyeing, and sewing the cloth. Producing silk was so important that the Empress of China always announced the beginning of the year's silk producing season.

FROM PULP TO PAPER

The Egyptians made a writing material from the papyrus plant around 3000 B.C. The Chinese invented paper as we know it around 100 B.C. when they made a thick, uneven kind of paper from pulped fibers. However, they wrote their documents on bamboo paper or silk, even though bamboo was heavy and silk was expensive.

PAPERMAKING

Paper was made using fibers from a variety of sources, such as the hemp plant, the bark of the mulberry tree, bamboo, and even old fishing nets. The fibers were boiled to soften them and then pounded in water with a wooden mallet to make a pulp. A mold, consisting of a bamboo frame holding a grid or sieve of coarsely woven cloth, was then lowered into the pulp. After a while, the grid was removed, together with a thin sheet of pulp that had become attached to it. The frame was carefully pressed to remove excess water, then hung up to let the sheet of paper dry thoroughly before it was peeled away.

There are several papermaking stages: mixing the material, mashing and pounding the mixture, dipping a fine screen into the mixture, hanging the screen on a heated wall, and then peeling off the dry paper.

A monk wrote this poem in ink on a hanging scroll of paper in the fifteenth century A.D.

海客和尚龍阜退院之一
有一偈寺游之嚴韻次祖婦
倶州焦隱之行色云顙靳
劉刋
杉如天馬謝塵羈遮莫
辭亭長笛吹重疊闌心
毎不住洛梅且瘦折残枝
奉浦心宗樂松穆新

In a later development, papermakers covered the mold with thin strips of bamboo, laced with silk or animal hairs. This allowed them to remove the sheet of pulp from the frame and reuse the mold right away—without waiting for the paper to dry.

INK AND BRUSH

Chinese calligraphers made ink from the burned remains of pine and other plants.

This sooty mixture was combined with glue to make an ink stick. When the ink was needed, the stick was ground against a hard stone or piece of pottery to make a fine powder that was mixed with water.

Adding various pigments, such as cinnabar for red and indigo for blue, made colored inks. The ink was applied to the paper using a fine-tipped brush made of wolf, goat, or badger hair. A calligrapher's brush was often highly decorated with fine carvings and would have been a treasured possession.

Calligraphy is an art in which the brush is held firmly and vertically between thumb and middle finger.

INVENTING QUALITY PAPER

The first paper was not good enough to write on. Traditionally, the man who invented better quality paper was Ts'ai (or Cai) Lun, an official in the Chinese Imperial Court. He is said to have created his paper using silk rags. He presented his invention to the emperor in A.D. 105.

THE PRINTING PRESS

A thousand years ago, books were rare because each one was written by hand. In fifteenth-century Europe, Johannes Gutenberg revolutionized the making of books when he invented movable type that could be reused on a printing press. But the Chinese had printed books 400 years earlier.

BLOCK PRINTING

The first printers cut blocks from wood and carved and inked their surfaces to print patterns on textiles and short religious texts on paper. The earliest record of printing was in A.D. 593, when the Emperor Wen-ti ordered Buddhist images and scriptures.

Block printing a book involved several stages. To begin with, the text of each page was written on a piece of thin paper that was then glued face down onto a wooden plate. The characters were carved out from the wood to make a printing plate for that page. Every page in the book required its own carved wood block. Once all the blocks were ready and arranged in sequence, they were inked and pressed on to paper.

A skilled block printer produced a thousand sheets a day. By the ninth century A.D., people could buy books from private dealers in parts of China, something that would not happen in the West for hundreds of years.

Blocks of Chinese movable type are kept in trays at the offices of the Seattle Chinese Post, *a newspaper in Seattle, WA.*

MOVABLE TYPE

The invention of movable type (type that can be moved and reused) has been credited to Pi Sheng around A.D. 1040. Each piece of type had a single Chinese character carved in relief on a small block made of a mixture of clay and glue. The carved blocks of type were hardened by firing and could be used over and over again, whenever the character on its type was needed for a book. The printer had many blocks of type and all the Chinese characters—5,000 or more—he needed.

To print a book with movable type, the printer first smeared an iron plate with a mixture of paper ash, turpentine, resin, and wax. He arranged the blocks of type on the plate in the correct order to form the text of the book to be printed. They were held in place on the plate with iron fastenings. When the frame was full, it was placed near a fire to make the glue at the back of the type melt slightly. The printer pressed down the type

The Diamond Sutra *is the world's first printed text. It was printed in* A.D. *868.*

with a smooth board to make it as even as possible. The frame of type was then ready for printing. After, the plate was reheated to remove the blocks of type, which were then stored away in wooden frames.

MANY CHARACTERS

Printing didn't have the same impact in China as it did later in the West. One reason for this could be the complexity of the Chinese language, which requires thousands of separate characters, compared to the 26 letters of our alphabet. Using movable type didn't seem practical to the Chinese, so they abandoned the idea.

POTS AND PORCELAIN

Pottery was of great importance in China and the influence of Chinese porcelain on the work of potters in the West has been huge. In fact, China has played such an important role in the history of pottery that we now refer to fine white stoneware as china.

EARLY POTTERY

Pottery has been made in China for almost 15,000 years. Remains from 12000 B.C. reveal that potters worked with hand-shaped coils of clay, sometimes smoothed with wooden paddles, to make bowls and jars. Patterns were made by wrapping cords around the paddles or by marking the clay with tools. The clay was fired in a dome-shaped kiln built above a firebox.

The potter's wheel was probably developed in several places and was used in China around 2000 B.C. A heavy stone wheel set on a pivot was made to spin rapidly, allowing the potter to shape rounded, symmetrical vessels with delicate, thin walls.

Kilns were built with many small vents between the firebox and kiln. These helped to prevent ash from blowing up into the kiln and to spread the heat more evenly.

PRIZED PORCELAIN

During the seventh century A.D., Chinese potters discovered how to make porcelain while experimenting with different materials and techniques. True porcelain, sometimes called hard-paste porcelain, was a combination of kaolin, or China clay, and a mineral called feldspar, or China stone. The Chinese

This blue and white jar with the image of a five-clawed dragon was made in the eighteenth century.

The tomb of Qin Shi Huangdi contains thousands of soldiers made of terra-cotta.

called these two ingredients "the body and the bone" of the porcelain. Porcelain, unlike pottery, is translucent, which means that a strong light can be seen shining through it.

The main porcelain factory in China was at Jingdezhen in Jiangxi Province. At their height, these imperial potteries employed around a million people and were equipped with 3,000 kilns. The pottery they produced had glazes and decorations that were inspired by natural colors—a pale gray represented moonlight, while one called "cracked ice" conveyed the reflection of a sunny blue sky in the ice of a stream cracking with the first spring thaw.

THE TERRA-COTTA ARMY

An example of the Chinese mastery of ceramics can be seen in the Terra-Cotta Army, which was placed in the tomb of Qin Shi Huangdi, the First Emperor, in 210 B.C. The army consists of 6,000 life-size and lifelike figures made of terra-cotta, a kind of red clay. Each figure is a unique individual with its own distinct facial features. There were also horses with bronze and leather bridles, chariots of wood and bronze, iron farm implements, spears, swords, bows, and arrows.

Local craftsmen who normally produced drainage pipes from terra-cotta made the figures with the help of other laborers. They set up production lines to manufacture the various parts of the soldiers, assembling them after firing in kilns. The terra-cotta soldiers were then arranged in formation in the tomb according to their duties.

23

WORKING WITH BRONZE

Around 4000 B.C., people learned how to make bronze, which is an alloy of copper and tin. No one knows exactly when or where this discovery took place. Perhaps it was in China because there is plenty of tin there. The earliest bronze object from China, a knife found in Gansu province, dates from around 3000 B.C.

FROM POTTERY TO METAL

Around 2000 B.C., Chinese potters developed very efficient kilns that metalworkers realized could reach temperatures high enough to smelt copper from its ore.

Later, metalworkers discovered that adding tin to the copper lowered the melting point and produced a metal—bronze—that was harder and more durable than copper by itself.

Two-handled bronze vessels called gui *were used in rituals for food or wine. This* gui *was made about 3,000 years ago.*

Bronze smelting became very important during the Shang Dynasty (ca. 1766–ca. 1045 B.C.). Vast amounts of bronze were produced to make ritual objects for ceremonial purposes, wine vessels, musical instruments, food containers, and weapons for the army. Many bronze objects were engraved with records of the military exploits of Chinese rulers, which are extremely valuable for historical research.

PIECE-MOLD CASTING

The Chinese rarely hammered metal into shape as the Europeans did. Bronze articles were usually made by casting the molten metal in molds.

The Chinese developed an unusual method of casting bronze. First, they made a clay model of the object and carved the decoration on it. They let this model harden and then pressed soft clay against it to form a mold of the decorated object. The mold was removed in sections, revealing the model again. Next, they shaved a layer of clay from the model as thick as the vessel being made.

The pieces of the clay mold, carrying an impression of the model inside, were reassembled around the shaved-down model. Molten bronze was poured into the space between the mold and the model. Once it had cooled, the mold pieces were removed, ready to be used again. Because of the accuracy with which the models and molds were made, very little work was needed to complete the piece.

BRONZE INDUSTRY

Casting an object uses more metal than hammering one out. To make large numbers of bronze vessels and other objects, the Chinese must have mined and transported huge quantities of copper and tin.

Many people were involved in producing molds and smelting metal, and many more were involved in transporting the bronze goods where they were needed.

This elephant is a bronze wine vessel, or zun. *At the tip of its uplifted trunk is a crouching tiger and the head of a phoenix. The body is covered in clouds and other patterns.*

Working with Iron

Iron may first have been smelted in furnaces called bloomeries around 2000 B.C. in places such as India and the Caucasus, south of Russia. These furnaces were not hot enough to make molten iron that could be cast into objects. In China, people were making objects from cast iron as early as 400 B.C.

Blast Furnaces

How did the Chinese cast iron so long before the rest of the world? The answer was that they knew how to make blast furnaces that generated enough heat to produce molten iron. Cast-iron objects were not made in Europe until the Middle Ages.

Two Secrets

The Chinese knew two secrets about making iron. They invented a type of bellows, called the double-action piston bellows, that blew a continuous stream of air into the furnace. Other types of bellows only produced puffs and allowed the furnace to cool between each push on the bellows.

Another secret of iron production was to add black earth, which contained phosphorus. The Chinese discovered that this reduced the melting point of iron from 2,066°F (1,130°C) to 1,742°F (950°C). This temperature was much easier to reach in the blast furnace.

Drinking tea has always been important to the Chinese, so they made many kinds of teapots. This iron teapot has a spout in the shape of an elephant's trunk.

IN THE FURNACE

The furnace was fed with iron ore, crushed limestone, and coke or charcoal. The molten metal flowed out from the bottom of the furnace into a large stone trough where, in a difficult and dangerous task, it was stirred with rods of iron to make it stronger and easier to shape.

Around the third century B.C., Chinese iron workers discovered the technique of annealing. By heating the iron to a high temperature and cooling it slowly, they made the metal less brittle and easier to flatten with a hammer.

IRON TOOLS

Making tools and utensils with cast iron had many advantages over hammering iron. Swords were made longer and pots became thinner and, therefore, lighter. Farm implements, such as plowshares and sickles, were completely made of iron. Even towers called pagodas were assembled from cast-iron stories that were made separately.

An iron lion stands in front of Lama Temple, a Buddhist temple in Beijing.

IRON LION

In A.D. 954, the Emperor Shih Tsung instructed his ironworkers to make what is now known as the Great Lion of Tsang-chou. Made from a single piece of cast iron, it weighs around 44 tons (40 t) and stands 20 feet (6 m) tall.

TRAVELING ON LAND

Horse-drawn carts and carriages were the main forms of transportation in ancient China. The Chinese introduced innovations such as the harness and stirrup that are still, in one form or another, used today.

A HARNESS FOR HORSES

The earliest farmers all over the world had learned how to harness oxen and use their strength. People tried to harness horses in the same way, but this practically throttled the animal when it tried to pull a heavy load.

In about the fourth or fifth century B.C., the Chinese invented a harness that put the strain on the horse's breast rather than its throat. Later, they developed the neck collar, which allowed the horse to use all its strength when pulling. This invention did not reach Europe until the ninth century A.D., where it transformed farming.

MEASURING DISTANCE

Around the fourth century A.D., some carriages in China were fitted with a type of odometer, a device for measuring a distance traveled, which the Greeks invented independently.

A horse wearing a breast strap harness (a and b) was much more efficient when pulling a load. The neck collar (c) made plowing easier in different kinds of terrain.

(a)

(b)

(c)

A cast-iron stirrup is essential for the horseriders of the Taklamakan Desert in China.

twin stirrups dates from the early centuries A.D. Considering that people had been riding horses for thousands of years, it is puzzling that stirrups were not invented sooner.

A pair of stirrups, which gave the rider stability, is often considered to be an important invention because stirrups made it possible to ride horses in warfare.

A wooden figure connected to the wheels by a series of gears beat a drum with every 100 revolutions of the carriage's wheels. Because the wheels had a circumference of about 16 feet (5 m) each drumbeat meant roughly 1,600 feet (500 m) traveled.

RIDING STIRRUPS

The saddle was invented around 800 B.C., possibly by the Assyrians. Before this, riders probably used a single loop of leather on one side of the saddle to help them mount a horse. The first real evidence of

THE WHEELBARROW

The wheelbarrow used on building sites and in gardens throughout the world was invented in China around 200 B.C. It was easy to handle and could be pushed along flat surfaces or hills. The wheelbarrow was economical and practical and was used to carry goods or even people.

THE COMPASS

People all around the world use a compass when they want to find out the direction of north, south, east, or west. The oldest type of compass, and the one with which we are most familiar, is the magnetic compass. We can trace its invention back to China.

The ancient Chinese used this compass to help them shape the landscape.

A CHANCE DISCOVERY

No one knows when the magnetic properties of a type of iron ore—called magnetite or lodestone—were first discovered. Perhaps it was some time between about 700 and 500 B.C., when Chinese miners who were searching for copper and iron ores found by chance that magnetite attracted iron. They also discovered that if they allowed a piece of magnetite to move freely, it would point in a north-south direction.

We tend to think of a compass as pointing north, but the Chinese came to call it a "south-pointer." By about 200 B.C., they were using a spoon-shaped compass made of lodestone that sat on a plate of bronze. The handle of the spoon pointed south. The Chinese were very interested in knowing which direction was south because they believed that the entrances to their homes should always face south for good fortune.

By the seventh century A.D., the Chinese had discovered that they could make compasses by rubbing iron needles with magnetite to

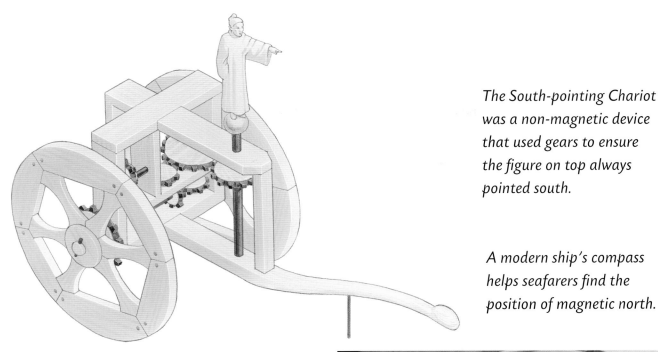

The South-pointing Chariot was a non-magnetic device that used gears to ensure the figure on top always pointed south.

A modern ship's compass helps seafarers find the position of magnetic north.

magnetize them. The needles were suspended in water so that they could turn freely. They also discovered that if they kept a red-hot needle pointing in a north-south direction (the direction of Earth's natural magnetic field), it became magnetized as it cooled.

THE COMPASS GOES TO SEA

At first, the magnetic compass may simply have helped sailors check the direction of the wind when clouds or fog hid the sun or the stars. From about the tenth century A.D., Chinese sailors used the magnetic compass to successfully navigate their way as far away as Saudi Arabia.

The use of the compass spread rapidly across the world. Western European sailors were using it by 1187, the Arabs by 1220, and the Scandinavians by 1300. Whether or not the discovery was passed on by the Chinese is unknown. It is possible that all of these seafaring people discovered their own version of the compass independently.

FINDING THE WAY

The earliest mention of magnetism was found in a Chinese book from the fourth century B.C. called the *Book of the Devil Valley Master.* This book says: "When the people of Cheng go out to collect jade, they carry a south-pointer with them so as not to lose their way."

Traveling on Water

Around 10,000 years ago, the Chinese people were making canoes and rafts. They built ferries, water taxis, and flat-bottomed boats called sampans for traveling on rivers, canals, and waterways. Eventually, they built ships called junks that became "the kings of the sea" and traveled across the Yellow Sea and into the ocean.

Humble Beginnings

Early Chinese boats were like two dugout canoes joined together with planks of wood to form a raft. The sides, bow, and stern were built up with more planks of wood so that the boat resembled a large, flat-bottomed wooden box that floated on water.

A wedge-shaped addition to the bow of the boat helped it to move more easily through the water. From these humble beginnings, the Chinese developed an assortment of water craft for short journeys and junks for longer trips. Junks can still be seen sailing the waters around China today.

The Chinese Junk

Chinese junks were first made around 200 B.C. At their peak around the tenth century A.D., they were the biggest ships in the world. The largest junks may have been 460 feet (140 m) long, with four to six enormous sails. Such ships were five times the size of the largest ship Christopher Columbus sailed across the Atlantic Ocean in 1492.

This eighteenth-century painting on silk shows the Emperor Yang Ti (A.D. 560–618) on his boat on the Grand Canal in China.

A junk sails in Victoria Harbor, Hong Kong.

The sails of a junk were made of panels of linen or matting flattened by bamboo strips. Each sail was spread and closed by pulling on ropes, similar to opening or closing a Venetian blind. This made them much simpler to operate than the complex rigging of European ships. The sails were also much more maneuverable, allowing the junk to sail into the wind.

Inside, the hull of the junk was divided into 12 or more waterproof compartments by solid bulkheads. This not only gave the junk additional strength, but also made it difficult to sink. The massive rudder of a junk took the place of a keel and its flat bottom enabled it to sail safely in waters that were too shallow for ordinary keeled ships.

THE RUDDER

The earliest means of steering a ship was a large paddle or oar at the stern. This became the steering oar—Greek and Roman ships usually had two sets of steering oars, one mounted on each side. Chinese shipbuilders took a different approach. They built a watertight box that held the rudder and extended through the deck of the ship at the stern. This allowed them to place the rudder on the centerline of the ship and gave them far greater control over steering.

OLD RUDDERS

The oldest representation of a ship's rudder can be seen on a pottery model of a Chinese ship dating from the first century A.D. The oldest evidence for rudders on European ships was found in a carving on the font in Winchester Cathedral dating from around the year 1180, a thousand years later.

TIMEKEEPING

The Chinese, like people of other cultures, keenly observed the movements of objects in the sky, such as the sun, moon, planets, comets, meteors, and stars. They believed that the movements of these heavenly bodies were linked to events on Earth.

From the sixteenth century B.C. on, government officials were charged with recording the changes seen in the heavens.

The first recording of a meteor shower was in 2133 B.C. The first reliable report of a solar eclipse was recorded by Chinese astronomers on May 26, 1217 B.C. The first sighting of Halley's comet was recorded in 613 B.C.

CLOCKS AND TOWERS

The Chinese built various mechanical timekeeping devices as models of the astronomical movements. For example, third-century Chinese *clepsydras*, or water clocks, drove various mechanisms that demonstrated astronomical events.

The Chinese scientist Su Sung built one of the most elaborate clock towers in A.D. 1088. Known as the "cosmic engine," Su Sung's clock tower stood more than 33 feet (10 m) tall and included a water-driven escapement.

This stone sundial stands in the Forbidden City, Beijing.

34

The moon shines through the rings of an armillary sphere at the ancient observatory in Beijing.

INCENSE ALARM CLOCK

Around the tenth century A.D., the Chinese determined the time with candles and sticks of incense that burned down at a steady rate. These devices, cast in bronze, were often shaped like dragons. A sequence of bells was tied to threads that were evenly spaced on incense sticks. When the incense burned through a thread, a bell fell down, indicating that a specific length of time had passed.

The escapement was invented by the Chinese around 725 A.D. It is the part of a clock or watch that that ticks. The escapement, which works with the balance or pendulum of the timepiece, determines its accuracy.

At the top of the clock tower, there was a bronze model of the movements of objects in the heavens. This is called an armillary sphere. It showed the position of the sun, moon, and certain stars. This helped to determine the Chinese calendar as well as making astrological predictions.

Doors on the five front panels of the tower opened to reveal wooden figures that rang bells or gongs to announce the time of day.

All the mechanisms in the tower were powered by the water wheel inside.

MEASURING THE YEAR

Chinese scientist Guo Shoujing (1231–1316) created a tower sundial, which stood 43.73 feet (13.33 m) tall. By taking careful measurements of the changing shadow cast by the tower, he calculated that there were 365.2425 days in a year—just 26 seconds different from the time it takes Earth to go around the sun.

Around 1600, astronomer Xing Yunlu built a 65-foot (20 m) tall sundial and calculated the year's length even more accurately—to within 2.3 seconds of measurements made with modern scientific equipment.

TRADITIONAL CHINESE MEDICINE

The system of medicine that evolved in China is very different from the one that developed in Europe. Traditional Chinese medicine diagnoses illnesses by checking pulses in the wrist and looking at the condition of the tongue, urine, and skin. Its treatments include herbalism and acupuncture.

TAKING THE PULSE

A key part of Chinese thought is the idea that two opposing forces—*yin* and *yang*—influence the world and need to be kept in balance. A person developed a disease or illness when their *yin* and *yang* were not in harmony, either within them or in their environment.

To discover the balance of a person's *yin* and *yang*, a Chinese doctor assesses the pulses at the wrist. There are 24 different kinds of pulse, including *fu* (floating), *hua* (smooth), *jin* (tense), and *xu* (feeble). From their knowledge of these pulses, Chinese doctors can judge the condition of their patients and establish how severe an illness might be.

HERBAL REMEDIES

Chinese doctors had a great knowledge of herbal remedies for many conditions. A handbook from the second century A.D.

Angelica is an ancient herbal remedy for easing indigestion.

recorded 365 remedies for treating conditions that included asthmatic coughs and malaria.

ACUPUNCTURE

Acupuncture dates back to before 2500 B.C. It is still practiced today, not only in China but also as an alternative therapy throughout the world.

According to Chinese medical thought, the body contains 12 channels, or meridians, along which the life force, or

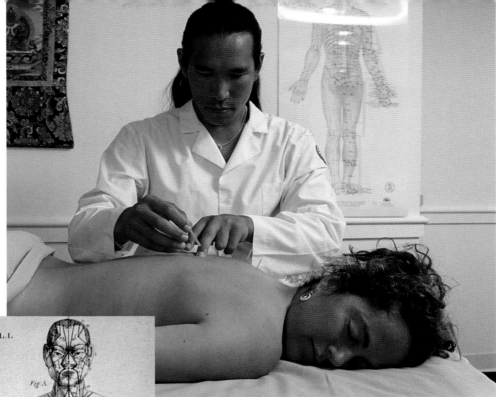

An acupuncturist places needles in the skin of a patient.

This acupuncture chart shows the meridians and acupoints in the human body.

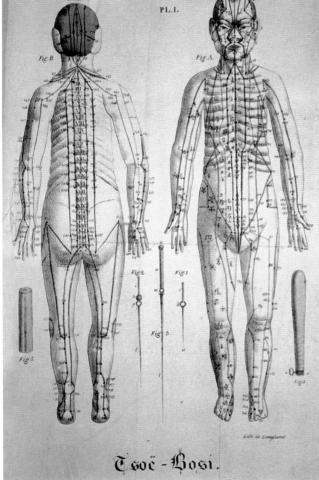

treatments can be done by precisely inserting one or more fine needles into the skin at particular points called acupoints on the meridians. The needles used in acupuncture are from 1 to 9.5 inches (2.5–24 cm) long.

chi (pronounced chee), flows. One goal of Chinese acupuncture is to influence the flow of *chi* in the meridians after a diagnosis has been made—for example, to unblock it or to speed it up. Another aim is to affect the condition of the organs of the body. These

RARE SURGERY

Surgery was rare in ancient China because people believed the human body should be respected. However, Hua Tuo, a surgeon who lived in the second century A.D., carried out abdominal surgery. He used an anaesthetic herbal mixture called *mafeisan*, which the patient took dissolved in wine. After Hua Tuo's death in A.D. 208, his works were destroyed and little progress was made in the field of surgery.

MILITARY TECHNOLOGY

In the history of China, there have been many wars. Battles were fought by rival states for control of cities. These sometimes involved hundreds of thousands of men, including cavalry, charioteers, bowmen, and infantrymen in armor.

A repeating crossbow was not very strong, but it could fire arrows rapidly —as many as 10 in 15 seconds.

THE CROSSBOW

Crossbows were one of the most important weapons in the armies of China at least as early as the fifth century B.C. Chinese crossbows were developed to help with rapid firing rather than to increase fire power, as they were in the West.

The advantage of the crossbow was that the bowstring could be pulled back using a lever mechanism and held ready on a trigger. A bowman with a bow and arrow had to use muscle power to hold his bow ready, so he was likely to tire sooner.

SIEGE WARFARE

One of the most important objectives for an army is to gain control of an enemy's cities. For thousands of years, the Chinese

PROPAGANDA WARFARE

After surrounding a city, attackers used arrows to fire leaflets over the walls. These offered rewards to people who surrendered peacefully and warned of the dire consequences for those who decided to fight. When this tactic failed, as it almost always did, the attackers turned to their catapults and other siege weapons.

built walls of pounded earth to protect their cities. An attacking army had to find a way to penetrate these walls. One method involved the fork cart. This had a long pivoting beam with a claw on the end that was swung into the city wall to break it down. A variety of catapults were also used to hurl large rocks at the walls.

Another tool available to attackers was a wheeled cart covered with oxhide that protected them from the defenders' arrows as they approached the city walls.

FLAMETHROWERS

By the tenth century A.D., Chinese armies were using flamethrowers. They used the pumping technology that operated their blast furnaces to produce a continuous stream of "fierce fire oil." As it left the barrel of the flamethrower, the stream was lit by a slow-burning gunpowder match.

When the four-wheeled fork cart was moved into position, the long-armed claw chopped away at the earth walls.

At the Battle of Wolf Mountain River in A.D. 93, Qian Yuan-guan defeated the enemy fleet by burning their ships with with fire oil. The fire oil was probably a mixture of petroleum and other substances such as quicklime.

GUNPOWDER

The world would be very different today if there were no explosives. We would still be fighting wars, but without guns, cannons, bombs, and rockets they would be far less destructive. As with so many other things, the Chinese were the first to make explosives.

Gunpowder enabled cannons to fire heavy balls. This cannon defended a gorge on the Yangtze River.

FIRE MEDICINE

Chinese alchemists mixed together different compounds, hoping to discover the secret of eternal life. They may have stumbled on gunpowder by chance some time around the seventh or eighth century A.D., when an experiment blew up unexpectedly.

Gunpowder is a gray powder, a mixture of saltpeter (potassium nitrate), charcoal, and sulfur—it was quite unlike anything anyone

had ever seen before. A flame caused it to explode with a bright flash and a loud bang, producing clouds of foul-smelling smoke. The alchemists called the mixture "fire medicine."

FIREWORK DISPLAY

At first, the Chinese used gunpowder in fireworks for religious festivals and official ceremonies. Bamboo tubes filled with gunpowder were thrown onto fires to make impressive bangs. The idea for making rockets may have come when a tube that failed to explode was propelled out of the fire by the gases produced by the burning gunpowder.

Rockets and Bombs

In the eleventh century, the Chinese used gunpowder more and more in warfare. By the thirteenth century, the Chinese Bureau of Munitions had seven factories producing 7,000 rockets and 21,000 bombs a day. These weapons included the thunder-crash bomb. The Chinese first used this bomb in 1232 to fight Mongol troops who attacked the city of Kaifeng in northern China.

Fire arrows were the first true rockets. A tube, capped at one end, was filled with gunpowder and mounted on a long stick. When the gunpowder was ignited, the gas escaping from the open end of the tube propelled the fire arrow through the air. The stick kept

The Fire Lance

The pear-flower spear, or fire lance, was one of the earliest weapons to use gunpowder in battle. A small gunpowder charge under the head of a long spear shot out a small projectile or poison at the enemy. The fire lance had a range of only a few feet and was effective in close combat, but it was an important first step in the development of firearms.

the rocket stable as it flew through the air. However, we do not know how much damage was caused by these terrifying fire arrows.

Explosive fireworks light up the sky in Tiananmen Square in Beijing.

CHINESE TIME LINE

ca. 3500 B.C.   The earliest Chinese city is built at Liang-ch'eng chen.

ca. 2600 B.C.   Silk production begins in China.

ca. 1600 B.C.   The first city-based civilization is established in China; the Bronze Age culture is established.

1550–1050 B.C.   The Shang Dynasty is the first Chinese dynasty to leave historical records.

ca. 650 B.C.   Iron working technology is introduced in China.

ca. 500 B.C.   The iron plow is invented in China.

ca. 200 B.C.   The collar harness for horses is invented in China.

ca. 100 B.C.   A multi-tubed seed drill is invented in China.

551 B.C.   Philosopher and teacher Confucius is born.

479 B.C.   Confucius dies.

ca. 221 B.C.   China becomes a united country, under the Ch'in Dynasty (from which China takes its name).

ca. 112 B.C.   The Silk Road, the great trading route between China and the West, opens.

ca. 100 B.C.   Blast furnaces are used in China.

A.D. **105**   Paper is first used in China.

A.D. **220**   China splits into three rival states.

ca. A.D. **270**   The magnetic compass is in use in China.

ca. A.D. **300**   The foot stirrup for horse riding is invented in China.

A.D. **304**   North China splits into a collection of barbarian states known as the Sixteen Kingdoms.

A.D. **589**   China is reunited.

ca. A.D. 593 Printing is introduced in China.

ca. A.D. 750 The technique of papermaking spreads from China to the Muslim world and on to Europe.

A.D. 868. The *Diamond Sutra* is produced in China. It is the first printed document for which a date of printing is recorded.

A.D. 874 A wave of peasant uprisings begins.

A.D. 907 China splits again; 10 kingdoms control different sections of southern and western China.

A.D. 947 The Khitans from Mongolia overrun northern China and establish their capital at Peking.

A.D. 979 The Sung Dynasty reunites China.

ca. A.D. 1000 The great age of Chinese painting and ceramics begins.

ca. A.D. 1040 Movable type printing is invented in China.

A.D. 1126 The Chin overrun northern China, restricting the Sung to the south.

A.D. 1234 The Chin empire is destroyed by the Mongols.

A.D. 1275 Marco Polo arrives in China.

A.D. 1279 The Mongols conquer southern China.

A.D. 1368 The Ming Dynasty is founded in China.

ca. A.D. 1405 Chinese sailors explore the Indian Ocean.

ca. A.D. 1500 Wan-Hu attempts rocket-powered flight but is blown up.

A.D. 1514 The first European traders since Marco Polo arrive in China.

GLOSSARY

alchemist Someone who practices alchemy, an early form of chemistry.

alloy A mixture of two or more different metals. Bronze is an alloy of copper and tin.

annealing A heating and cooling process that makes metal less brittle and easier to shape.

Assyrians The people of ancient Assyria, a kingdom between the Tigris and Euphrates rivers in what is present-day Iraq.

blast furnace A furnace for melting iron from its ore.

calligraphy The art of decorative handwriting.

cast iron Iron made by pouring molten iron into a mold.

chi The universal life force in Chinese belief.

clepsydra A device for measuring time by the steady flow of water.

cocoon A protective layer that an insect larva spins around itself when it is ready to become an adult.

coke A substance formed by heating coal to a high temperature in the absence of air.

durable Long lasting.

escapement A device in a clock that controls the rotation of its gear wheels.

filament A slender thread.

firebox The place in a furnace where the fuel is burned.

hull The main part of a ship including the bottom, sides, and deck.

junk A flat-bottomed Chinese boat.

keel The lengthwise central part of a hull that extends into the water to give extra stability.

kiln An oven for firing pottery.

lodestone A piece of naturally magnetic magnetite that can be used as a magnet.

magnetite A gray-black form of iron oxide that
is naturally magnetic.

moldboard The part of a plow that turns over the soil.

novae (plural of nova) Stars that increase suddenly in brightness.

pagoda A tower with several stories, usually part of a temple or monastery in China.

petroleum Another name for crude oil.

phosphorus A chemical element that ignites spontaneously when in contact with air.

plowshare The main blade of a plow.

porcelain A type of fine translucent pottery.

sampan A type of small Chinese boat.

sandstone A type of rock made of sand grains that have been squeezed together over millions of years.

sickle A harvesting tool with a short handle and sharp, curved blade.

smelt To extract metal from its ore by heating and melting.

spindle A slender rod used to wind up thread as it is spun.

spooling frame A frame onto which thread is wound.

stoneware A type of pottery that is fired to a higher temperature than earthenware.

translucent Something that lets light through.

treadle A lever worked by foot.

winnowing fan A fan that supplies a stream of air to help separate grain from the chaff.

yang In Chinese belief, the male part of the universe, associated with heaven, heat, and light.

yin In Chinese belief, the female part of the universe, associated with the earth, cold, and dark.

FURTHER READING

Ball, Jacqueline. *Ancient China: Archaeology Unlocks the Secrets of China's Past.* Washington, DC: National Geographic, 2007.

Shuter, Jane. *Ancient China.* Chicago: Raintree, 2007.

Waryncia, Lou, and Ken Sheldon. *If I Were a Kid in Ancient China.* Peterborough, NH: Cricket Books, 2006.

WEB SITES FOR KIDS

http://eawc.evansville.edu/chpage.htm
Discover more about ancient China and its culture with information on everyday life in ancient China and links to interactive games.

http://www.kidsnewsroom.org/elmer/infoCentral/frameset/civilizations/
In this virtual museum, click on China to learn more about its history, culture, and geography.

WEB SITES FOR TEACHERS

http://school.discoveryeducation.com/lessonplans/programs/greatwall/
This site features a lesson plan that follows the development of the Great Wall and the influence each dynasty had on its construction.

http://k12east.mrdonn.org/China.html
Visit this site for additional lesson plans and PowerPoint presentations about ancient China.

INDEX